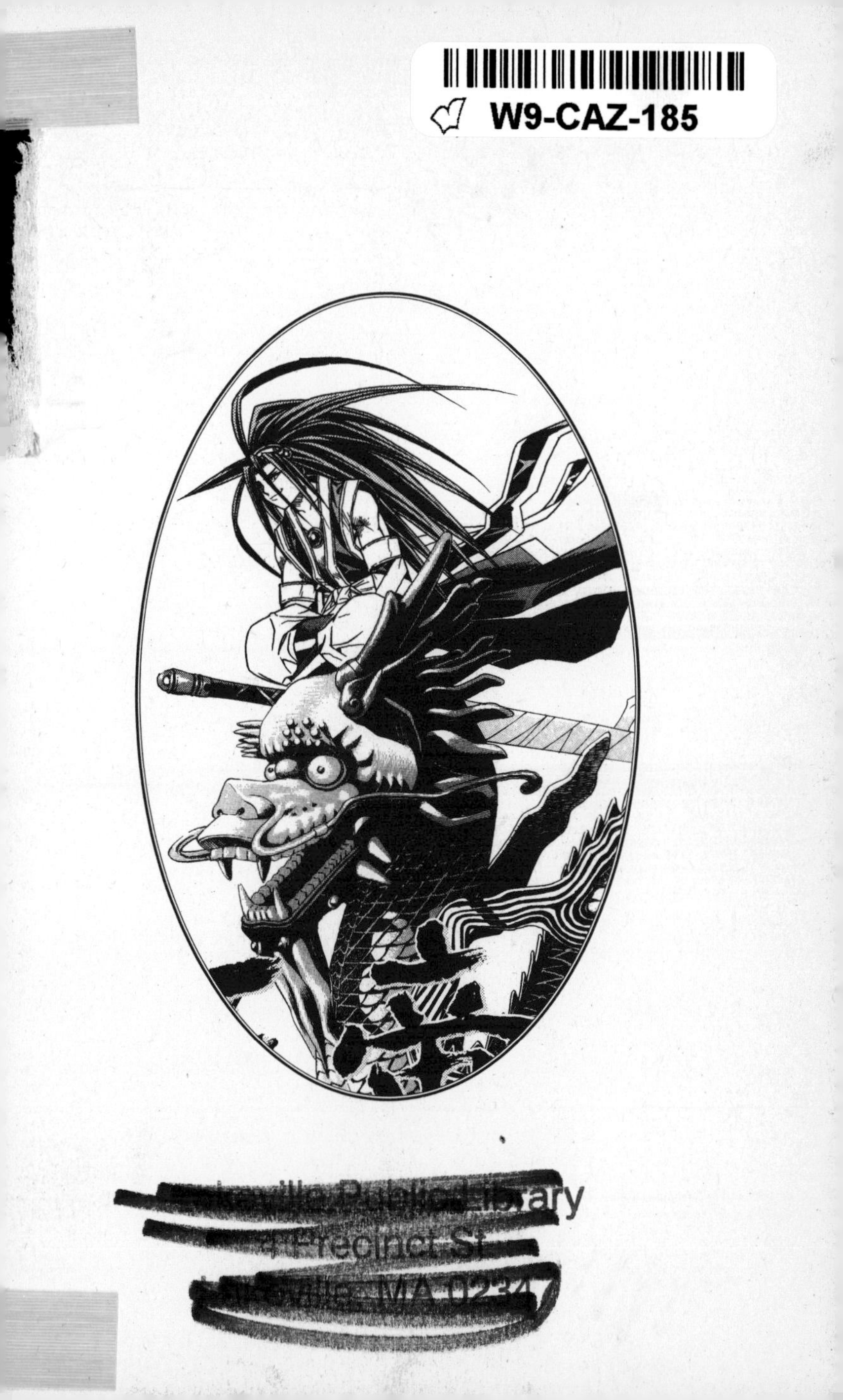

Translator - Lauren Na
English Adaptation - R.A. Jones
Copy Editors - Aaron Sparrow
Retouch and Lettering - Tom Misuraca
Cover Layout - Patrick Hook
Graphic Designer - James Dashiell

Editor - Rob Tokar
Digital Imaging Manager - Chris Buford
Pre-Press Manager - Antonio DePietro
Production Managers - Jennifer Miller, Mutsumi Miyazaki
Art Director - Matt Alford
Managing Editor - Jill Freshney
VP of Production - Ron Klamert
President & C.O.O. - John Parker
Publisher & C.E.O. - Stuart Levy

E-mail: info@TOKYOPOP.com
Come visit us online at www.TOKYOPOP.com

A TOKYOPOP® Manga

TOKYOPOP Inc.
5900 Wilshire Blvd. Suite 2000
Los Angeles, CA 90036

King of Hell Vol. 6

ISBN:1-59182-484-2

First TOKYOPOP printing: July 2004

10 9 8 7 6 5 4 3 2 1

Printed in the USA

Volume 6

By
Ra In-Soo
&
Kim Jae-Hwan

King of Hell™

Who the Hell...?

MAJEH:
A feared warrior in life, now a collector of souls for the King of Hell. Majeh has recently been returned to his human form in order to carry out the mission of destroying escaped evil spirits upon the earth. There are two catches, however:
1. Majeh's full powers are restrained by a mystical seal.
2. His physical form is that of a teenage boy.

CHUNG POONG NAMGOONG:
A coward from a once-respected family, Chung Poong left home hoping to prove himself at the Martial Arts Tournament in Nakyang. Broke and desperate, Chung Poong tried to rob Majeh. In a very rare moment of pity, Majeh allowed Chung Poong to live...and to tag along with him to the tournament. Chung Poong's older brother--Chung Hae--is also a student of the martial arts and is the "nephew" (martial arts inferior) of Poong Chun.

THE MARTIAL ARTS CHILD PRODIGIES

"BABY":
A mysterious, shy, 15-year-old from the infamous Blood Sect, his weapon is the deadly "snake hand" technique. Much to the relief of his fellow contestants, this fearsome ability hasn't yet reached full maturity...or has it? There's definitely much more to Baby than meets the eye!

CRAZY DOG:
A 6-year-old hellion wh
partial to using a club,
wild child hails fro
remote village...and he
nitely lives up to his nan

SAMHUK:
Originally sent by the King of Hell to spy on the unpredictable Majeh, Samhuk was quickly discovered and now--much to his dismay--acts as the warrior's ghostly manservant.

DOHWA BAIK:
A vivacious vixen whose weapons of choice are poisoned needles. She joined Majeh and Chung Poong on the way to the tournament.

KING OF HELL:
You were expecting horns and a pitchfork? This benevolent, otherworldly ruler reigns over the souls of the dead like a shepherd tending his flock.

)HAK:
15-year-old monk and
master at fighting with
od, he is affiliated with
Sorim Temple in the
ong mountains.

POONG CHUN:
A 12-year-old expert with the broadsword, he is affiliated with the Shaman Sect. Poong Chun is the "uncle" (martial arts superior) of Chung Hae--Chung Poong's older brother.

OUNG:
15-year-old sword-master,
ossessing incredible
peed, he is affiliated with
ooyoung Moon-- a clan of
sassins, 500 strong.

Story Thus Far

Hell's worst inmates have escaped and fled to Earth. Seeking recently-deceased bodies to host their bitter souls, these malevolent master fighters are part of an evil scheme that could have dire consequences for both This World and the Next World. It is believed that the escaped fiends are hunting for bodies of martial arts experts, as only bodies trained in martial arts would be capable of properly employing their incredible skills.

To make matters even more difficult, the otherworldly energy emitted by the fugitives will dissipate within one month's time...after which, they will be indistinguishable from normal humans and undetectable to those from the Next World. The King of Hell has assigned Majeh to hunt down Hell's Most Wanted and return them to the Next World...but Majeh doesn't always do exactly what he's told.

Majeh was a master swordsman in life and, in death, he serves as an envoy for the King of Hell, escorting souls of the dead to the Next World. Majeh caught Samhuk--a servant for the King of Hell--spying on him and, after making the appropriate threats, now uses Samhuk as his own servant as well.

The King of Hell has reunited Majeh's spirit with his physical body, which was perfectly preserved for 300 years. Due to the influence of a Superhuman Strength Sealing Symbol (designed to keep the rebellious and powerful Majeh in check), Majeh's physical form has reverted to a teenaged state. Even with the seal in place, however, Majeh is still an extremely formidable warrior.

Along with the young, wannabe-warrior called Chung Poong Namgoong and a beautiful femme fatale named Dohwa Baik, Majeh has made his way to the heralded

Martial Arts Tournament at Nakyang--the most likely place for the warrior demons to make their appearance.

Shortly after arriving in Nakyang, Majeh and company met Chung Hae--Chung Poong's older brother--though it was far from a happy reunion. Chung Hae berated his younger sibling and ordered Chung Poong to return home. To make matters worse, Poong Chun--Chung Hae's "uncle" (his superior in martial arts)--arrived and berated both siblings. Never one to miss an opportunity to make a new enemy, Majeh intervened and publicly shamed Poong Chun. Unsurprisingly, Poong Chun's vow to get even failed to impress Majeh in any way.

With the start of the tournament, Majeh's behavior only got more outrageous as he easily bested his first opponent. Chung Poong was well on his way to his first victory over the hulking 13-year-old Abaek until Chung Poong succumbed to his worst enemy: his own fear. After the fight, even the ultra-insensitive Majeh was consoling Chung Poong...until Chung Hae dropped by with a heaping helping of scorn for his younger brother. Always happy to give as good as he gets, Majeh delivered an extremely humiliating (and painful) defeat to Poong Chun when they met in the tournament.

Now, the Martial Arts Tournament continues with Young slated to fight Baby and Majeh facing Crazy Dog! Though Majeh seems to have forgotten his mission to capture Hell's Most Wanted, the escaped evil souls have certainly not forgotten him!

When Majeh's prey is on the hunt for their hunter, does even Hell's cockiest envoy have a hope against a force of pure evil?

와
와
와
와

헉
ABAEK! WHAT--?
HI. NICE TA SEE YA AGAIN, CHUNG POONG.

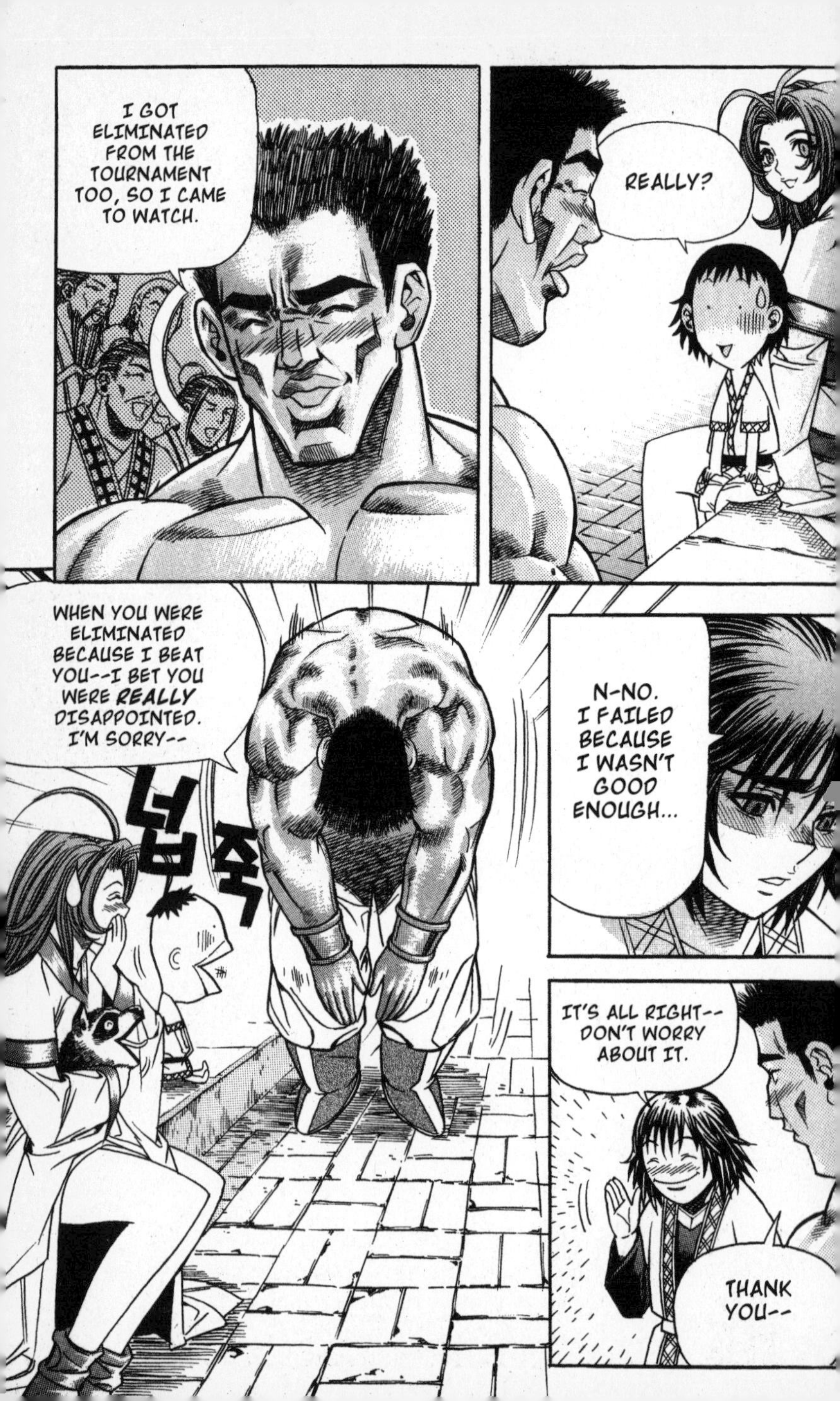
I GOT ELIMINATED FROM THE TOURNAMENT TOO, SO I CAME TO WATCH.
REALLY?
WHEN YOU WERE ELIMINATED BECAUSE I BEAT YOU--I BET YOU WERE *REALLY* DISAPPOINTED. I'M SORRY--
넙죽
N-NO. I FAILED BECAUSE I WASN'T GOOD ENOUGH...
IT'S ALL RIGHT--DON'T WORRY ABOUT IT.
THANK YOU--

EY!
WHAT?!
HUH! WHAT DO YOU THINK I AM--CRAZY LIKE YOU, CRAZY DOG?!
GIVE IT UP, MAJEH.
I WARN YOU...I WON'T LET ANYONE GET BETWEEN ME AND MY LOVE--I MEAN, MY FUTURE!
...

꿈틀
...
빡
GET READY!
BRING IT ON!
까딱

AMAZING!
T SWORD
MENT WAS
AST--BUT
ONE THEY
L "BABY"
STILL ABLE
OID BEING
'S THAT THE
THEY CALL
E SHAPE
ONVER-
SION?
NO?
NO...IT ISN'T.
THAT'S...
..THE *PHANTOM TECHNIQUE*. IT'S A LETHAL ECHNIQUE USED BY THE *BLOOD ECT*. A PHANTOM SER IS NEITHER EARD NOR SEEN!

THAT BABY-FACED BOY...
HE'S USING THE PHANTOM-- ONE OF THE LETHAL TECHNIQUES OF THE BLOOD SECT.
THAT WOULD MEAN THAT HE'S THEIR FAMED PRODIGY!
IF THAT'S SO...
...THEN WHO IS THE BOY FIGHTING CRAZY DOG!?

YOU... ASTARD...!
I'LL TEAR YOU APART !!

AMAZING!
C'MON, POOCH--

SURELY...
...YOU CAN DO BETTER THAN *THAT*!

I'LL KILL YOU!!
ZZZZZ

YOU THINK I'M SCARED OF A PUNK WITH THE SOUL OF A DOG?
GROWL ALL YOU LIKE...I'VE ALREADY WON.
......

KING OF HELL

KING OF HELL

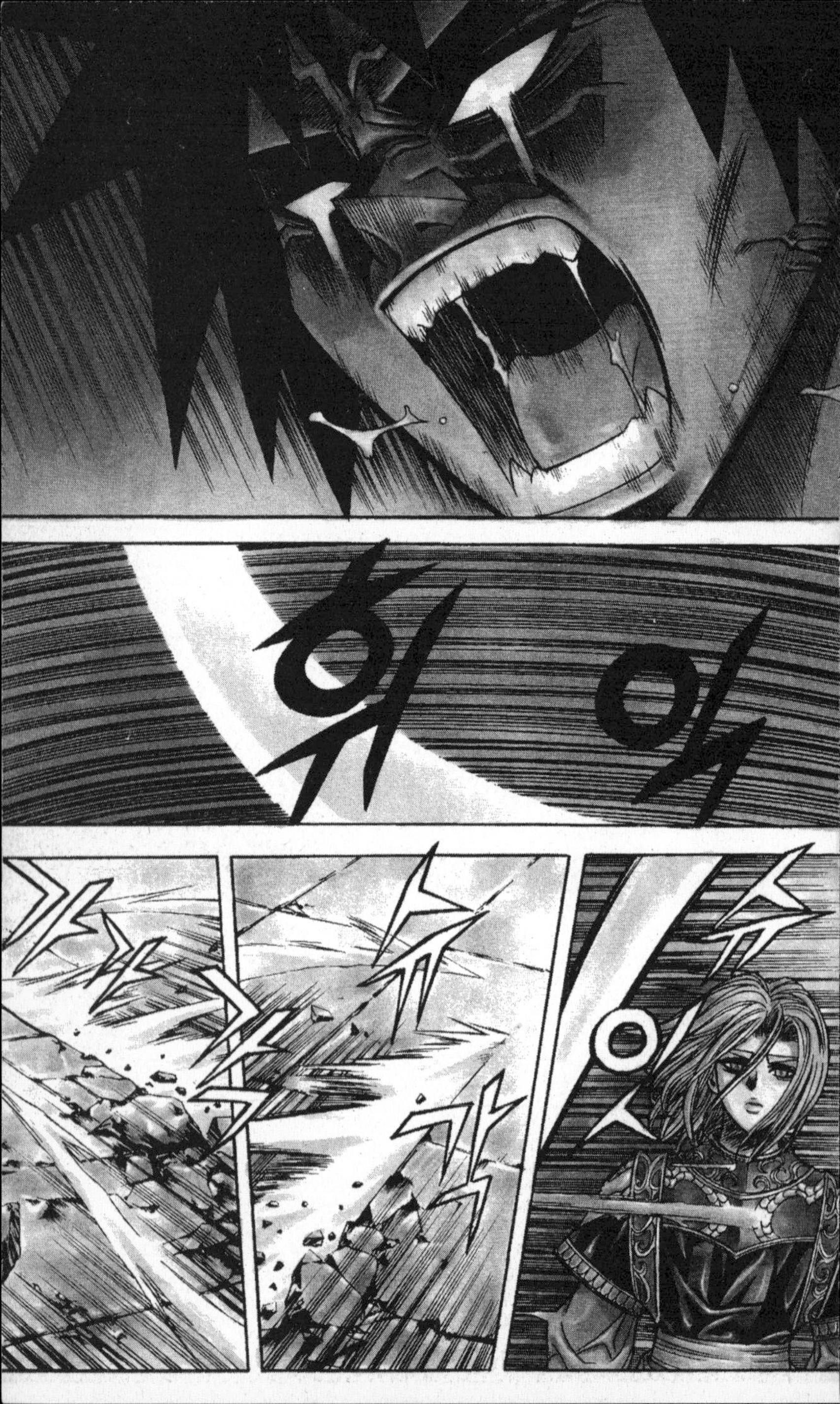

핫 앗

휘릭
빙글
빙글

......
UH...THAT'S THE ONLY THING I KNOW **HOW** TO DO, **YOUNG**...
HOW LONG DO YOU INTEND TO EVADE ME, BABY?!

......!
ARE YOU PLAYING ME FOR A *FOOL*?
NO... NO, I'M NOT. I REALLY...
WHAT
NSENSE...

ALL RIGHT, THEN...I'LL JUST HAVE TO COME UP WITH AN ATTACK YOU CAN'T DODGE!!

WHAT'S YOUNG DOING? WHY IS HIS ARM SHAKING? DID HE HURT HIMSELF?
I'M SURE HE DIDN'T.
OH HO-- WE FINALLY GET TO SEE IT! THE MOOYOUNG MOON'S SPECIALTY--
THE CHOO SAL SWORD TECHNIQUE!

LET'S SEE IF YOU CAN EVADE ME NOW!
...!

THE CHOO SAL ECHNIQUE IS THE OOYOUNG MOON'S SPECIAL SSASSIN ORD SKILL!
IT IS KNOWN FOR ITS UNGODLY VELOCITY...

차핫

...!
...FORCE...

...AND ABILITY TO INSTANTA-NEOUSLY CHANGE DIREC-TIONS!!
I-I CAN' BELIEVE CAN CHAN DIRECTIO SO EFFOR LESSLY A THAT SPEE

AT A YOUNG AGE, THE MOOYOUNG MOON ASSASSINS ARE TRAINED TO ADAPT THEIR BODIES TO NATURE AND TO MOVE WITH DEXTERITY.
THUS...
...IN THE CHOO SAL TECHNIQUE, HE USER IS PUSHING THE AIR AND HAT'S HOW THEY CAN MAINTAIN SUCH SPEED WHILE ABRUPTLY CHANGING DIRECTIONS.

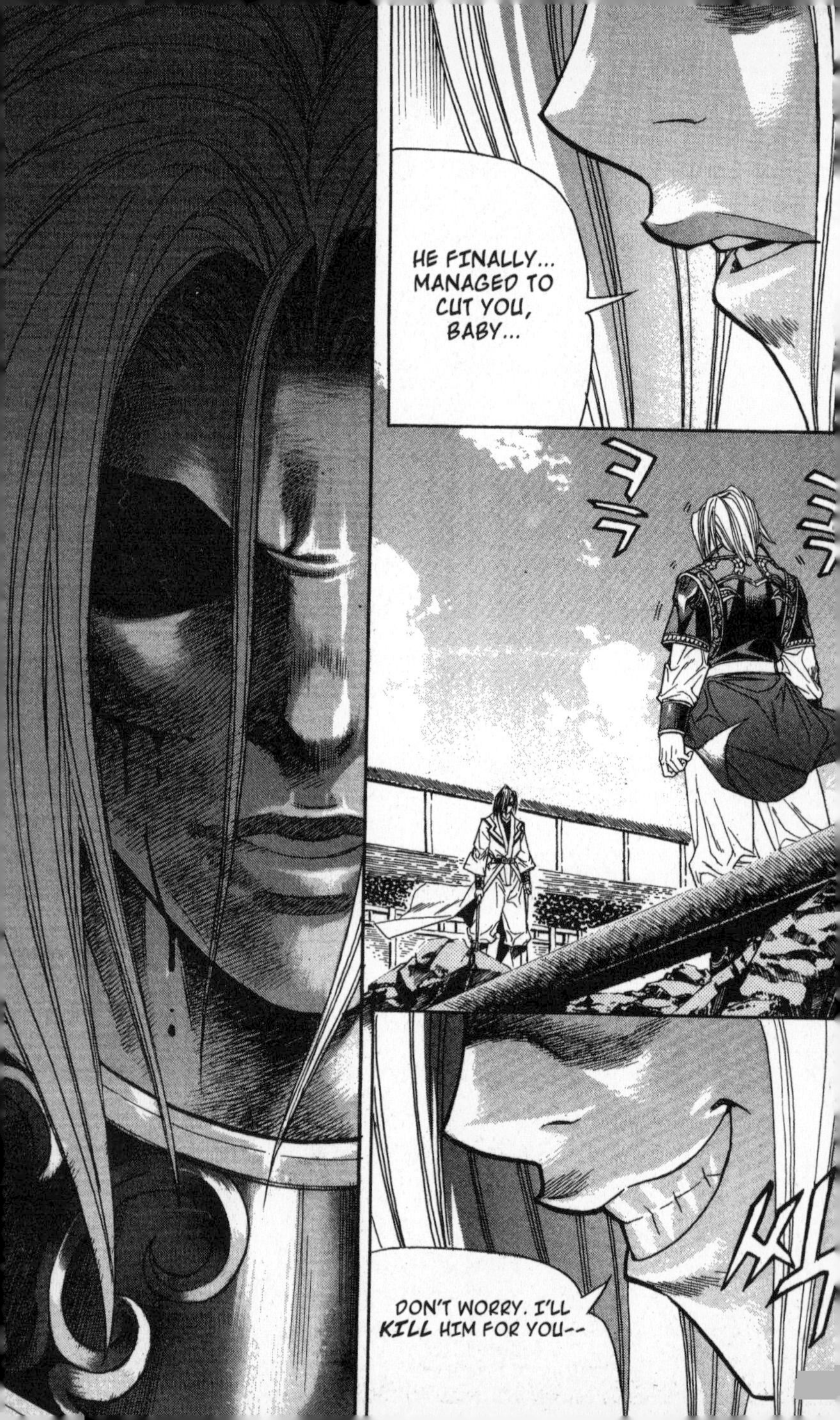

HE FINALLY... MANAGED TO CUT YOU, BABY...
DON'T WORRY. I'LL **KILL** HIM FOR YOU--

NO!
NO... STOP! DON'T DO IT, HYUR!
...
T'S TIME OR YOU O TAKE A ACK SEAT O ME--
--BABY!

WHAT'S GOING ON?
WHAT'S WRONG WITH HIM?
웅성
웅성
YOU... DO YOU, BY ANY CHANCE, HAVE...
MULTI
...PERSONALITIES ?!

I'M HYUR! HA HA--!
NICE TO MEET YOU.
AND UNLIKE BABY...I DO KNOW HOW TO ATTACK!

HEY, WHAT'S WITH THE FROWN? HA HA HA HA HA!
YOU...YOU ALREADY KNEW--DIDN'T YOU?
FROM THE VERY BEGINNING. DESPITE THAT SMILING FACE... YOU'VE BEEN EMITTING THIS INTENSE... MURDEROUS... ENERGY.
I WOULD HAVE BEEN A FOOL NOT TO HAVE NOTICED IT.

KING OF HELL

武林盟

YEAH-- WHAT ROTTEN LUCK.
LL THE DAYS BE POSTED OUTSIDE HE ARENA.
武林
LUCK HAS NEVER BEEN A LADY TO ME.
HA HA!

HUH?
YOU CAN'T GO IN RIGHT NOW, OLD MAN. ENTRANCE IS PROHIBITED ONCE THE COMPETITION HAS BEGUN, SO--
DO YOU THINK HE'S HERE TO WATCH THE COMPETITION?

!
AH...AH...!

武林盟

?
!
WHERE IS IT COMING FROM?
WHAT WAS THAT NOISE?

I SENSE AN ENERGY SOURCE... FROM THE NEXT WORLD!
OH, DEAR, YOUNG-- YOU FOUND ME OUT. AND HERE I WAS PLANNING ON ATTACKING YOU WHILE YOU WEREN'T LOOKING...
YOU'RE... A SNAKE HAND FIGHTER!

UNLIKE BABY -- I'M WELL PREPARED TO FIGHT...DON'T YOU AGREE?
...NOT REALLY...
!

WHAT ARE YOU UP TO, YOUNG?
MY SENSES ARE TELLING ME THAT IT WOULD BE A MISTAKE TO FIGHT YOU.
HUMPH!
HOW LIKE AN ASSASSIN-- RUNNING AWAY!
ALL RIGHT, THEN -- RUN! BUT WHAT SHALL I DO WITH ALL THIS ENERGY?

MUST I THROW IT AWAY?
WHAT A *WASTE* THAT WOULD BE!

THANK GOD! I THOUGHT I WAS GONNA DIE!
IT... IT STOPPED!

HOO HOO...!
I GUESS IT'S ABOUT TIM TO RETURN THIS BODY TO THE DOPE!
GASP!
짝
HYUR DID THIS, DIDN'T HE?! I'M SORRY, I'M REALLY SORRY!
굽신
MR. YOUNG--ARE YOU ALL RIGHT? PLEASE ACCEPT MY APOLOGY!
꾸벅

CRAZY DOG! GET AHOLD OF YOURSELF! I DON'T HAVE TIME TO PLAY WITH YOU ANYMORE!!
HUMPH!
!

WHO'S THA OLD MAN?
WHAT THE--?!
WHAT DOES HE THINK HE'S DOING?!
HOW NOISY!

AHHHHK!!
AHHK!
AHK!
......!

ARRRGH!!
NO, CRAZY DOG! STOP, YOU FOOL!!

KING OF HELL

크아아
탁
!

WHAT AN IMPUDENT LITTLE BOY.
SO EAGER TO DIE.
NO!!

WHAT--
WHAT'S
GOING
ON?!
웅성 웅성

I'VE BEEN LOOKING FORWARD TO ETING YOU--
MAJEH!

WHAT HAPPENED?! WHAT...WHAT'S GOING ON?!
WE MUST LEAVE HERE AT ONCE, MISTRESS!
HURRY
HAR HAR...! WHAT'S WITH THE FROWN, MAJEH? IS IT, BY ANY CHANCE--BECAUSE OF THIS DEAD BOY?
NO... IT DOESN'T MATTER TO ME WHETHER A BASTARD LIKE HIM DIES OR NOT!

WHERE DID
OU GET THAT
UMAN BODY,
DEMON?
HA HA HA! SO IT'S THIS *BODY* THAT HAS YOU CONCERNED!
WAS ITS *ORIGINAL* OWNER A *FRIEND* OF YOURS, PERHAPS?
쿵
NHAT?!
THERE'S BEEN AN *ATTACK*-- AND GUARDS HAVE BEEN KILLED?!
YES...YES, SIRE.

HOW MANY ATTACKERS ARE THERE?
IT'S...IT'S A... ONE-ARMED... OLD MAN...
...!
WHAT?!
IT APPEARS...
...THAT I'L HAVE TO PERSONAL ATTEND T THIS!

HOW PATHETIC!
TO THINK THAT THE LEGENDARY MAJEH, WHO CAUSED SUCH HAVOC IN THE NEXT WORLD-- WAS A MERE BOY!
WHAT... IS HE TALKING ABOUT?
I DON'T KNOW, DOHWA...
BUT WAIT... YOU'RE UNDER THE CONTROL OF A STRENGTH-SUPPRESSING SPELL NOW, AREN'T YOU?

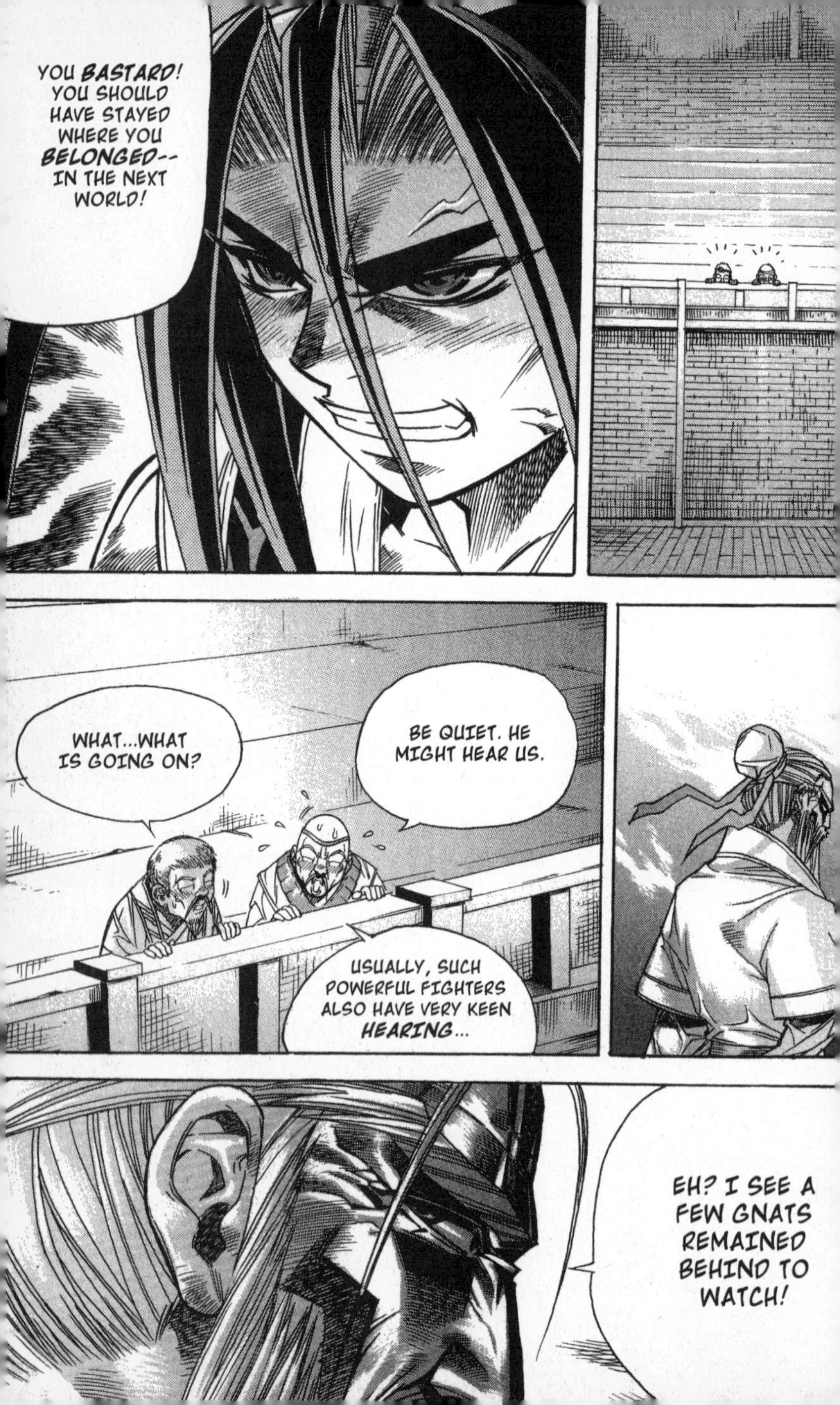
YOU BASTARD! YOU SHOULD HAVE STAYED WHERE YOU BELONGED-- IN THE NEXT WORLD!
WHAT...WHAT IS GOING ON?
BE QUIET. HE MIGHT HEAR US.
USUALLY, SUCH POWERFUL FIGHTERS ALSO HAVE VERY KEEN HEARING...
EH? I SEE A FEW GNATS REMAINED BEHIND TO WATCH!

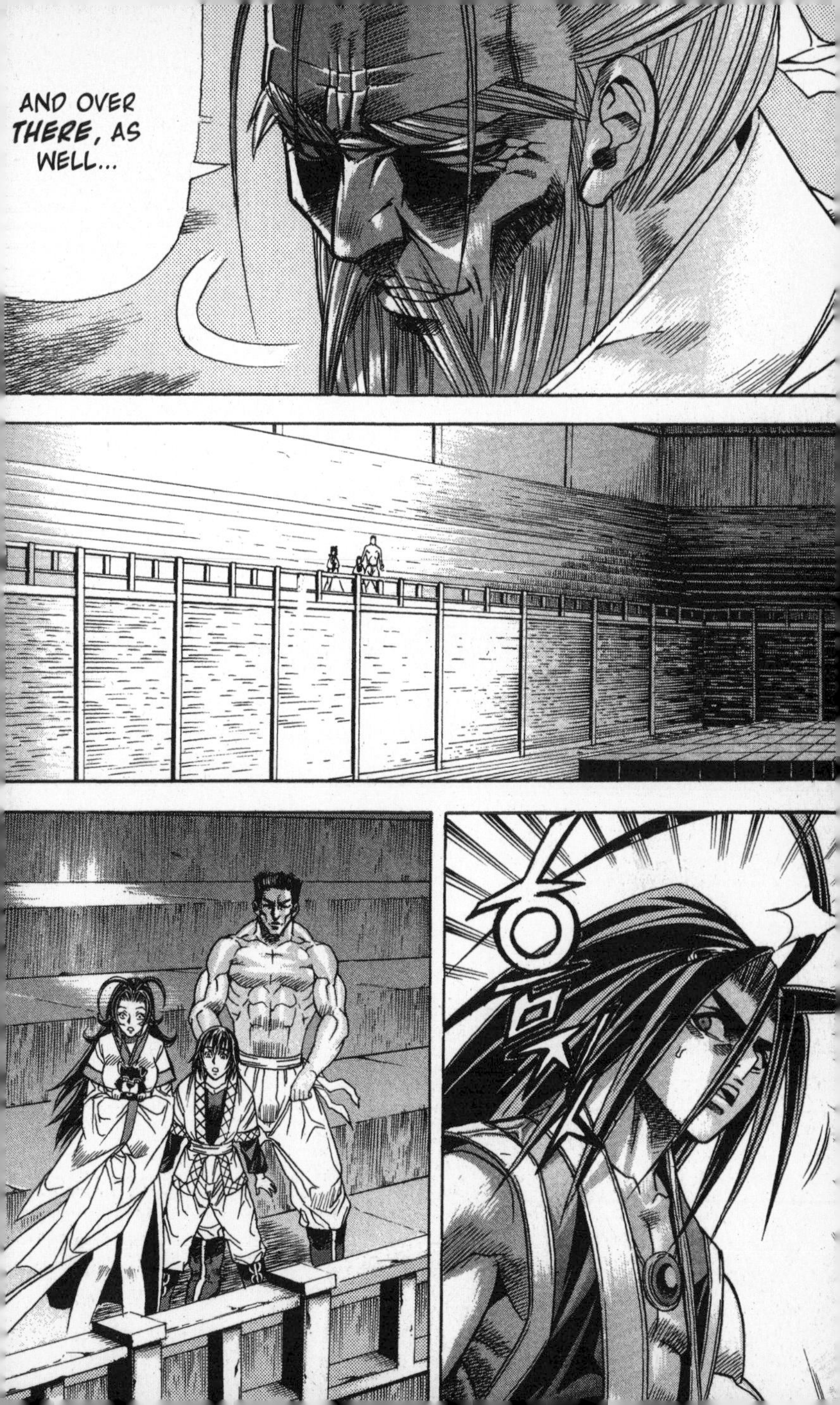
AND OVER THERE, AS WELL...

CHUNG POONG-- DOHWA! GET OUT!
M-MAJEH!!
GET OUT OF HERE-- NOW!!
OHO-- ARE THEY YOUR FRIENDS, MAJEH?! HOW REMISS OF ME... I HAVEN'T INTRODUCED MYSELF TO THEM YET!

NO!!
NICE TO MEET YOU!!

...!
ABAEK!

ABAEK...!
WHY SACRIFI YOURSEL FOR US
OH, NO...
WELL... I... I'M...

...NOT SURE...
MYSELF...WHY
I...DID...
IT...
ABAEK...!
!

ABAEK!
DON'T WORRY, LITTLE GIRL... THE BIG OX WON'T DIE **ALONE**!

KING OF HELL

OH, NO--IT WOULD BE TOO TRAGIC FOR HIM TO DIE ALONE!
LEAVE THEM ALONE, DEMON!
HO-- LEAVE T ALONE? AND W IF I REFUS
THEN I'LL KILL YOU!

WITH THAT BODY? DO YOU REALLY THINK YOU CAN?
I SWEAR...
...IF IT IS AT ALL POSSIBLE...
...MONSTER...

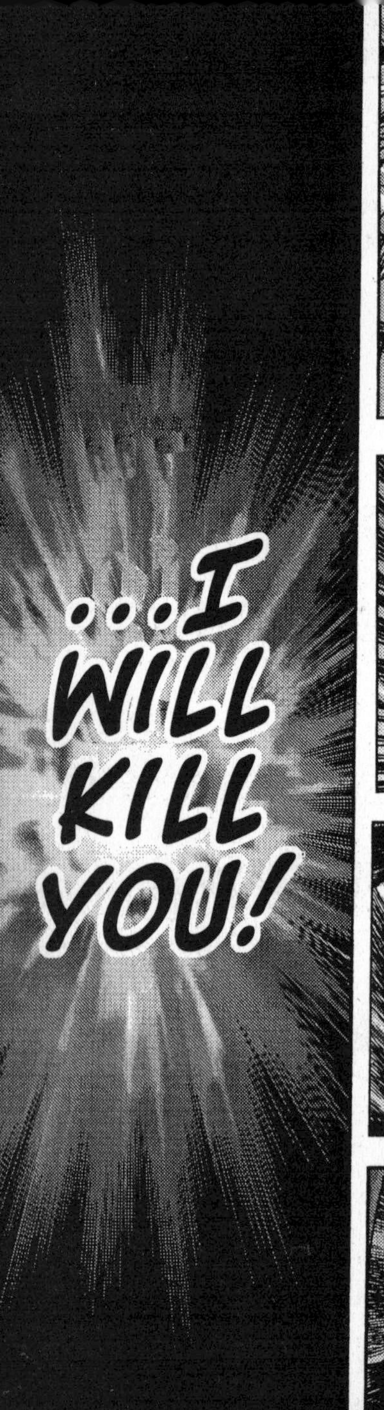
...I WILL KILL YOU!

HYAAA

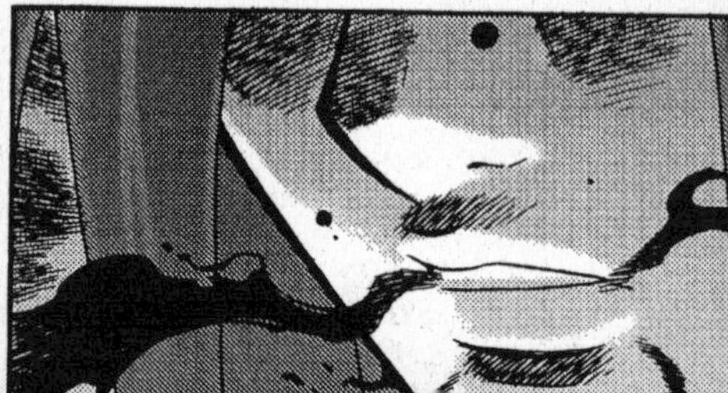

300
YEARS
AGO...
I SEE!

...THIS WAS THE SAME TECHNIQUE YOU USED...
...TO RUTHLESSLY CRUSH THE INHABITANTS OF MOORIM.

...SHOW ME HOW YOU DID IT...

...IF YOU CAN, BOY!
I'LL SHOW YOU, ALL RIGHT--
--BUT YOU WON'T LIKE WHAT YOU SEE!
WHAT...WHAT SHOULD WE DO, DOHWA?
FIRST, LET'S GET OUT OF HERE, CHUNG POONG. THIS AREA IS TOO DANGEROUS.
O-OKAY.

HOW LONG DO YOU PLAN ON JUST STANDING THERE, YOUNG MAJEH? ARE YOU TOO FRIGHTENED TO MOVE?

HARDLY!

IS THAT ALL YOU'VE GOT, DEMON?
THE SWORD IS BLOCKED BY THE HAND-- AND THE HAND IS BLOCKED BY THE SWORD!
UNBELIEVABLE!
IT'S A FIGHT BETWEEN TWO TITANS...

YOU'RE PATHETIC!
SHUT UP!

DAMN YOU!

KING OF HELL

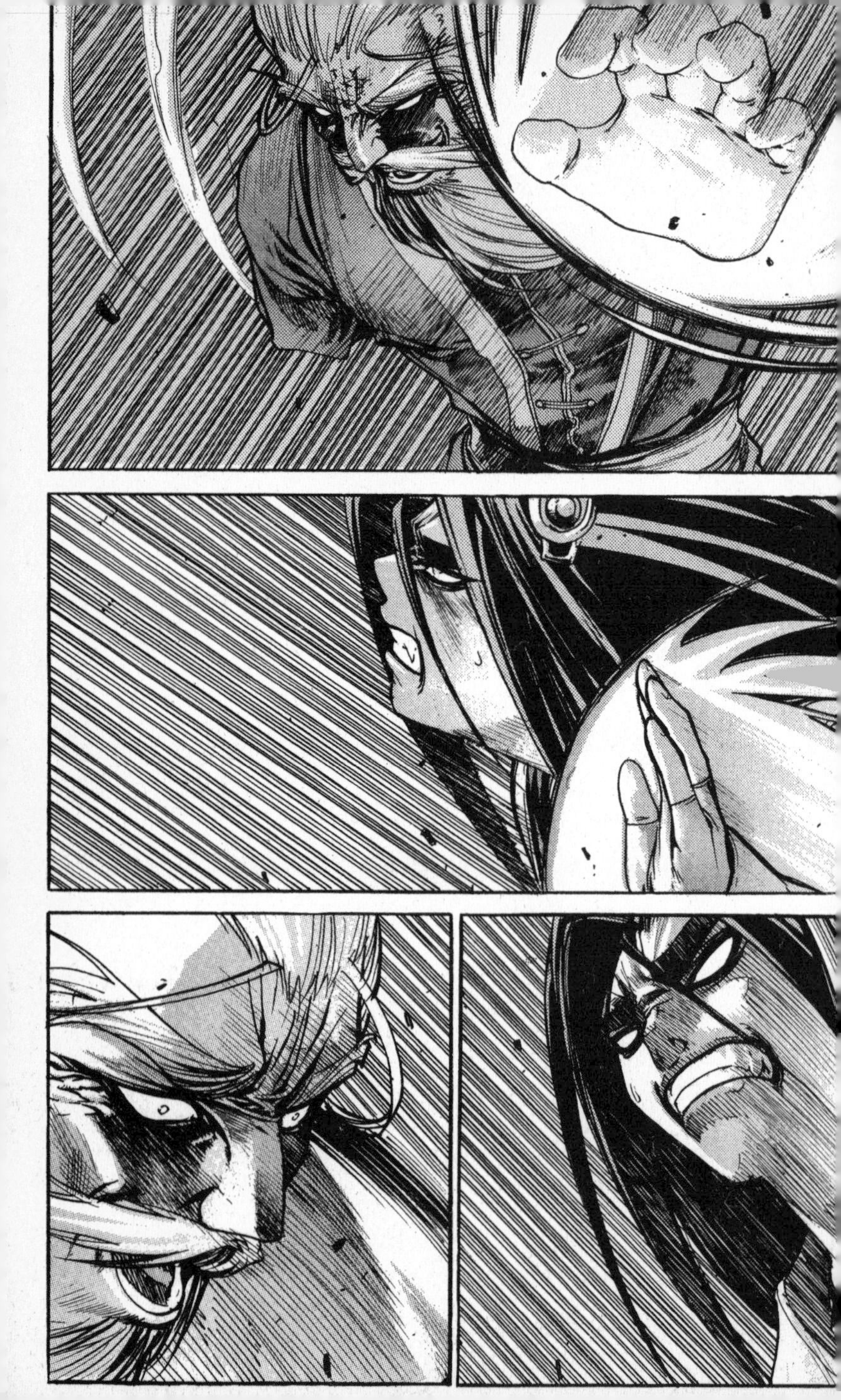

쾅
MAJEH!
ㅋㅋ

D-DAMMIT...
HOO HOO...! YOU WON'T BE USING THAT ARM FOR AWHILE.
AKE IT EASY N YOURSELF, AJEH. JUST SIT THERE QUIETLY...

...AND DIE!

SUCH INSOLENCE!

HAR!

HEH HEH...
THAT TICKLED!
!
IT'S HOPELESS FIGHTING WITH THIS BODY--EVEN THOUGH I'M USING EVERY FIGHTING TECHNIQUE I CAN MUSTER.
DAMMIT. IF IT WAS FOR THIS RESTRICTI SPELL I' UNDER, H WOULDN'T S A CHANC

퍽
UHK!
E'S FAST...

스읏
둥

WH-
WHAT?
BEG FOR YOUR LIFE, MAJEH!
IF YOU PLEAD ON YOU KNEES--
I'LL SPARE YOU!
HOO HOO!
LIKE HELL I WILL!

KHK!

COME ON, BOY...BEG FOR YOUR LIFE.
!

KING OF HELL

I'LL... NEVER... GIVE UP...
UH
STAY DOWN, YOU FOOL!
IF YOU CONTINUE T STRUGGLE LI THAT--YOU MIGHT JUS BREAK YOU NECK!!

R HAR!
E YOU
PAIN,
AJEH?
KHEEK!
STOP!
HUH?

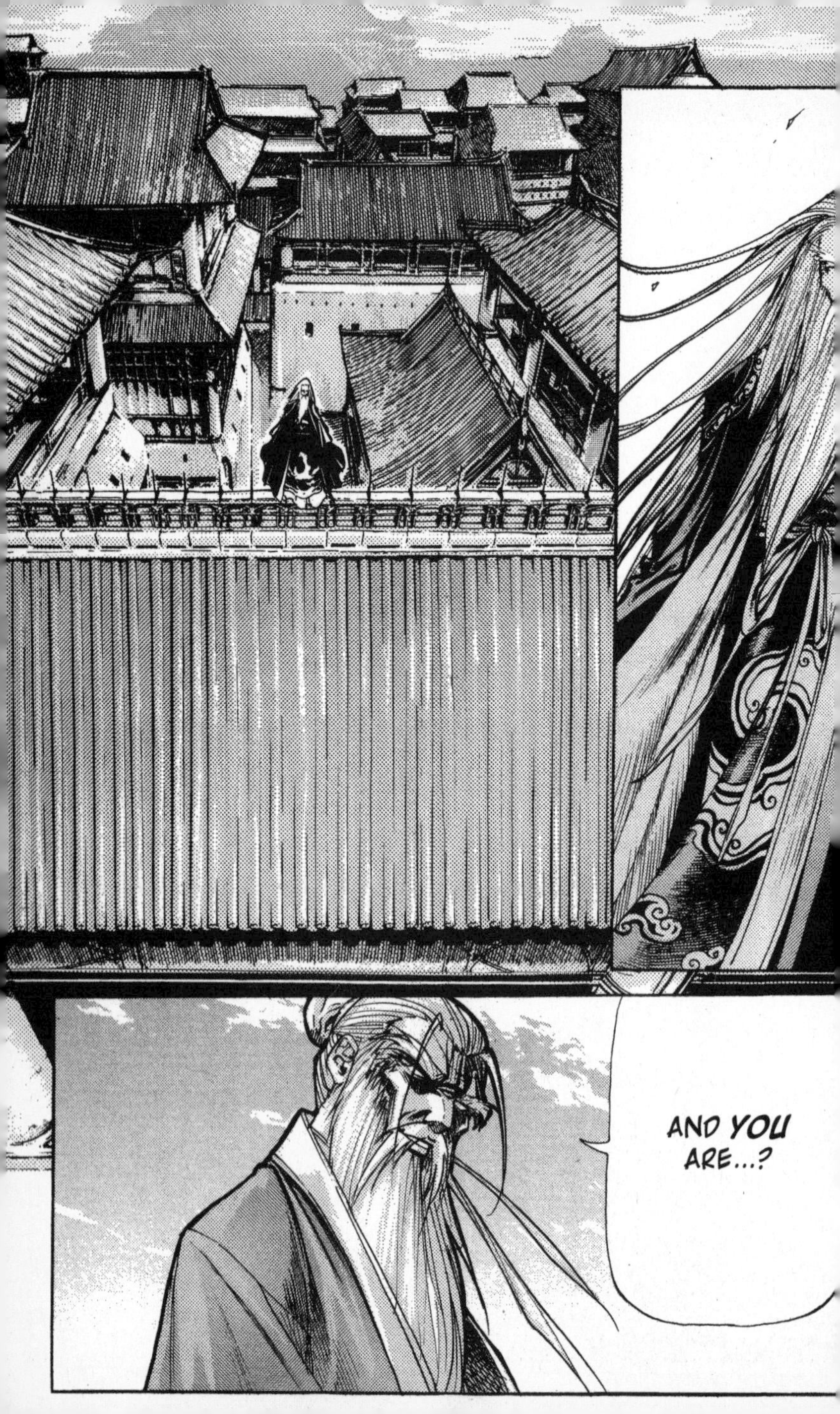
AND YOU ARE...?

I AM MO YOUNG--THE MARTIAL ARTS LEADER! I DON'T KNOW WHAT THE PROBLEM IS BETWEEN YOU AND THAT CHILD-- BUT YOU'VE GONE TOO FAR.
HOO HOO! THAT "CHILD"...
HEAR THAT, MAJEH?
AREN'T YOU AMUSED? A MAN MANY YEARS YOUR JUNIOR-- IS REFERRING TO YOU AS A CHILD!
KHK!
크 크..

HAR HAR! AND IF I DON'T: DO YOU ACTUALLY THINK YOUR PATHETIC SKILLS CAN STOP ME?
STOP THAT RIGHT NOW!

I FEEL AS IF I'M GOING TO SUFFOCATE JUST FROM THE ENERGY EMANATING FROM HIM!
HE'S RIGHT! I'M OBVIOUSLY NO MATCH FOR HIM!
WHERE IS THIS CREATURE FROM...?

...!
THIS IS A FIGHT THAT BEGAN WITHIN MY OWN HOUSE!
IF I STEP ASIDE NOW, MY REPUTATION AS THE MARTIAL ARTS LEADER WOULD BE--

STAY OUT OF THIS!
THIS IS A FIGHT BETWEEN ME AND HIM! I DON'T WANT ANYBODY BUTTING IN!

IF YOU INTERFERE, MO YOUNG-- I'LL MAKE YOU REGRET IT!
HA HA
HOW FUN
THE IRO OF Y THRE ENI SOME ELSE... YOU GROVE AT MY

IT'S OVER, BOY.

WHAT IS THIS...
...THIS...FEELING OF MISERY...
...OF... SHAME...?
DAMMIT!

NHAT IS HIS?!
HAVE YOU FINALLY REALIZED YOU CAN'T WIN, MAJEH?

AGH!

KING OF HELL

AAAAA!

HE'S GOTTEN FASTER!

AAAAH!

--HE'S EDIBLE, A! I THINK 'S GOING WIN!
YES...YES!

WHO IS THIS YOUNG BOY MAJEH...?
......
HOW CAN HE HAVE THAT MUCH POWER AT SUCH A YOUNG AGE?!
HE SUREL HASN'T LIV EVEN HAL A CENTURY- AND YET H **FIGHTS** LI AN **ANCIEN**

MAJEH HAS FOUGHT WELL...
BUT THE EVIL ONE STILL LIVES!

FROM THIS MOMENT ON-- YOU'LL NEVER KNOW FROM WHENCE I'LL STRIKE!

GAAAAA!
HOO HOO HOO!
HOW TIRESOME!
!

FACE ME!

IT'S BEEN A MOST ENJOYABL FIGHT, MAJE

KING OF HELL

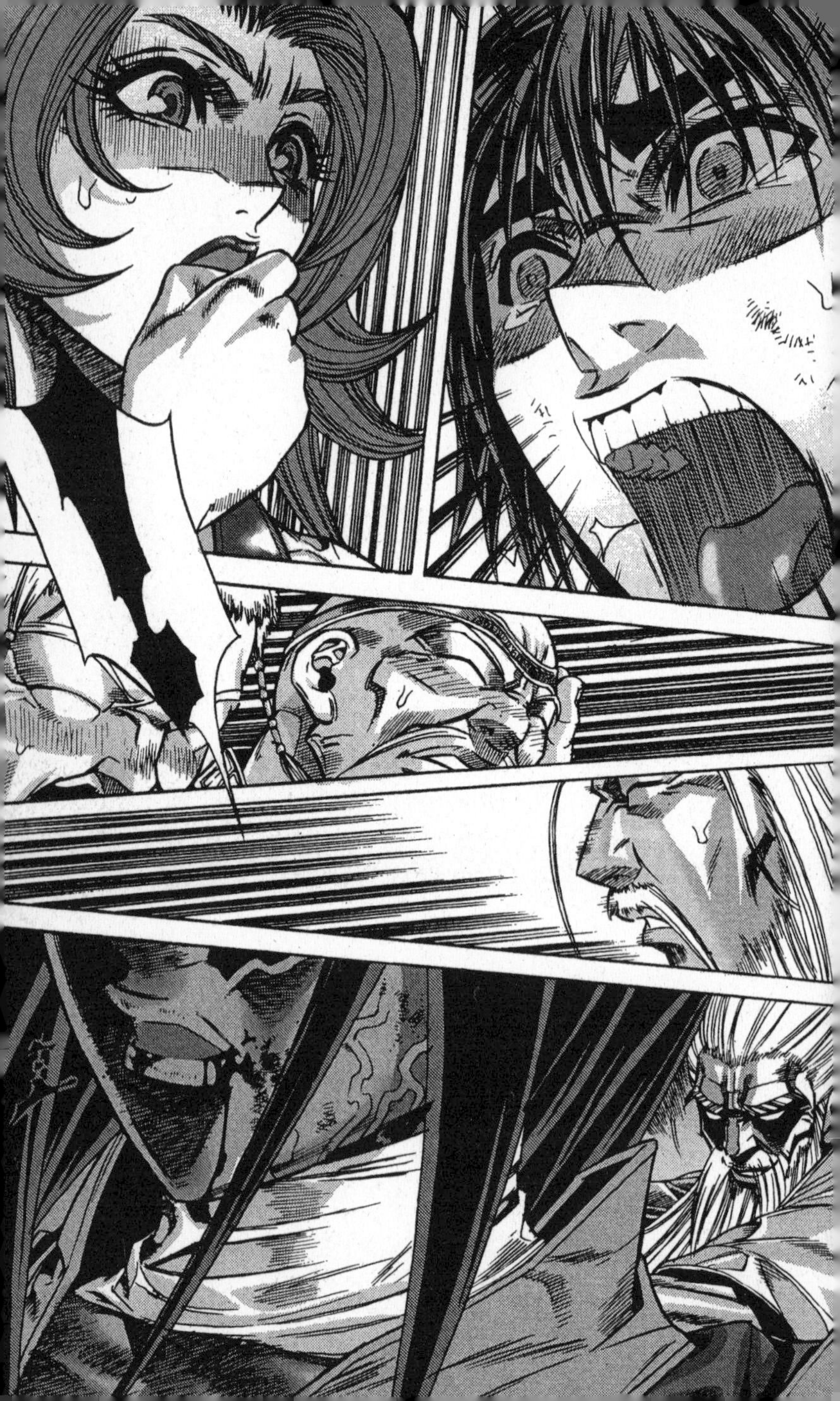

MAJEH!!
HEH HEH!

YOU'RE NO *MATCH* FOR US ESCAPED DEMONS... YET YOU THOUGHT TO *CAPTURE* US.

FOOL

WHEN YO
TO THE N
WORLD...
MY REGA
TO THE K

AH, I FORGOT... YOU TWO ARE STILL HERE.
HIS ENERGY REPELLED YOUR NEEDLES, DOHWA!
NOW WHAT?!
I COULD ET YOU TWO LIVE...
...BUT BECAUSE YOU'RE FRIENDS OF MAJEH'S... I WON'T!

HURRY, FRIEND--
LEAVE THIS PLACE.
YOU...
YOU'RE NOT
THINKING
OF...?
I'VE GOT
TO DO WHA
I CAN TO
SAVE THOS
YOUNGSTER

'RE NOT TRAINED FIGHT--SO YOU HOULD GO NOW!
...ALL HT. I'LL AS YOU SAY.
HEY-- *MO YOUNG*! ARE YOU GOING TO JUST STAND THERE AND WATCH HIM KILL THOSE CHILDREN?!

HOWEVER...IT APPEARS THAT OUR OPPONENT IS TOO POWERFUL!
WISE MAN? I THOUGHT THAT WAS YOU. I WAS JUST ABOUT TO TAKE ACTION.
SO?! OTHER THAN LOSING OUR LIVES-- WHAT'S THE WORST THAT CAN HAPPEN TO US?!
!

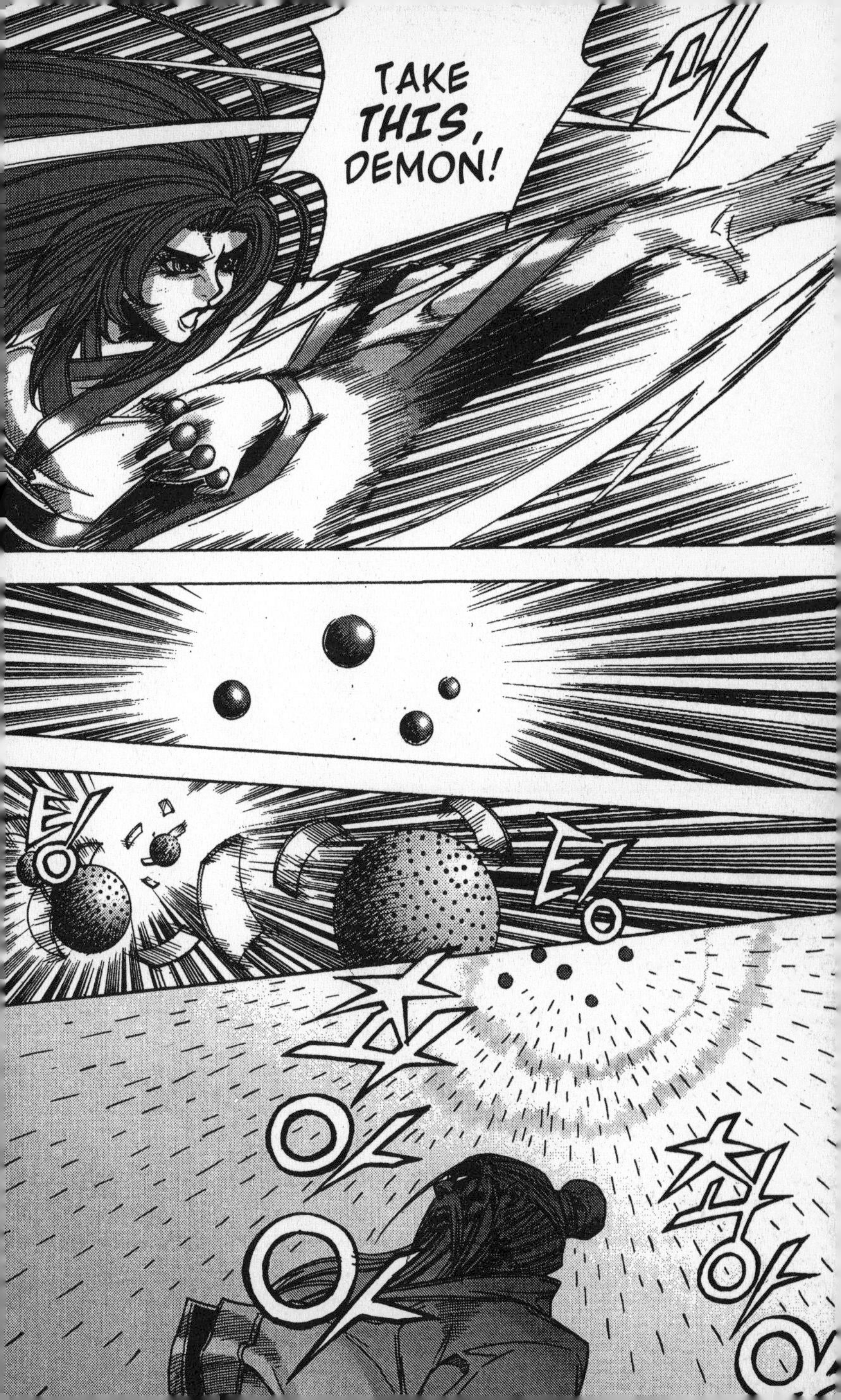
TAKE THIS, DEMON!

HYAAA!
!

HEH HEH!
DOHWA... WHAT ARE WE GONNA DO?
STAND FIRM AND PULL YOURSELF TOGETHER, CHUNG POONG!
A TRUE WARRIOR STANDS FIRM AND RESOLUTE. EVEN IF HE SHOULD DIE...AT LEAST HE CAN DIE WITH DIGNITY.
THE STRONG PREY UPON THE WEAK. THAT'S THE WAY OF NATURE--AND THAT'S THE WAY OF A WARRIOR!

SPOKEN TRULY, LITTLE ONE. SO...
...DIE!

HOW DARE YOU ATTAC THES CHILD ?!
HA!

IF YOU HIT ME, OLD MAN-- YOUR LEG WILL SIMPLY BREAK.
I DON'T THINK SO!
NO?
NO!

KING OF HELL

YOU...
PEST!

-ET'S SEE
F YOU CAN
ITHSTAND
HIS, EVIL
ONE!

IM-
IMPOSSIBLE...!
WAS THAT A *FEATHER* YOU STRUCK ME WITH, MO YOUNG?

THAT... MONSTER'S ELF-DEFENSE ENERGY FAR XCEEDS THE ACK STRENGTH THE MARTIAL RTS LEADER! IS IS WORSE THAN I EXPECTED...
HE'S TOTALLY OUT OF OUR LEAGUE!
YOU FOOLS JUST HAD TO BUTT IN.
NOW DIE!

KUHK!

HIS IS
RIBLE!
MAJEH'S SPIRIT HASN'T FLED HIS POOR BODY YET--
BUT IT'S ONLY A MATTER OF TIME.
I HAVE TO LEAVE--
--AND REPORT THIS TO THE KING OF HELL!

AAHH...
YOU TWO CHILDREN-
GET OUT OF HERE!
I'M AFRAID I CAN'T ALLOW THAT...

씨익

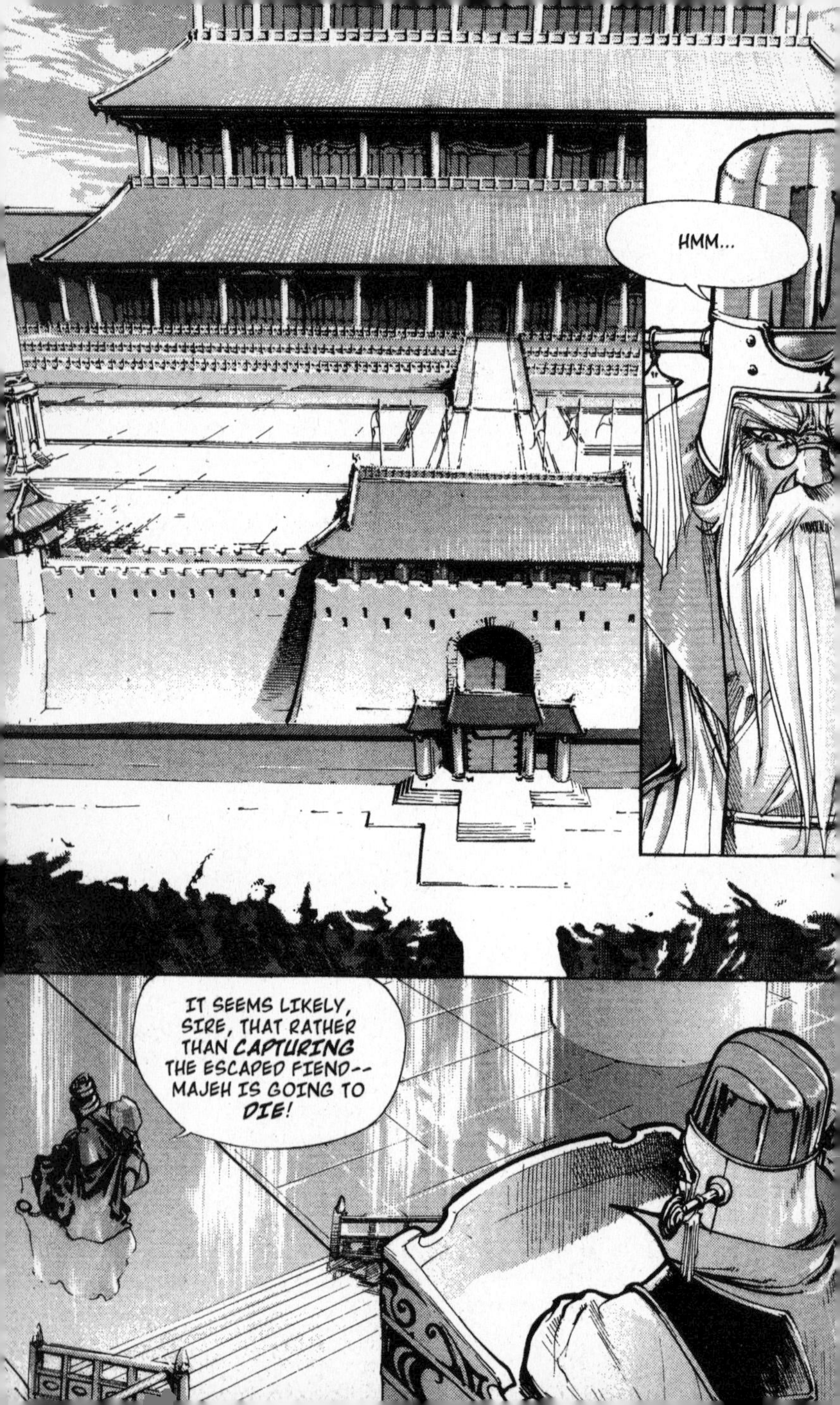
HMM...
IT SEEMS LIKELY, SIRE, THAT RATHER THAN CAPTURING THE ESCAPED FIEND--MAJEH IS GOING TO DIE!

RHAPS. WE'LL JUST HAVE WATCH AND SEE, LOYAL SAMHUK...
EXCUSE ME?! BUT NOTHING IS GOING TO CHANGE WITH US JUST WATCHING...!
THAT'S NOT TRUE!
THERE'S STILL A CHANCE.
..!
IT HAS TO DO WITH THE SPELL THAT WE CAST ON MAJEH TO SUPPRESS HIS SUPERHUMAN STRENGTH.

...
WHAT...WHAT ARE YOU SAYING, SIRE?
RISE...
RISE...

RISE...MAJEH.

DAMN...

DAMN...

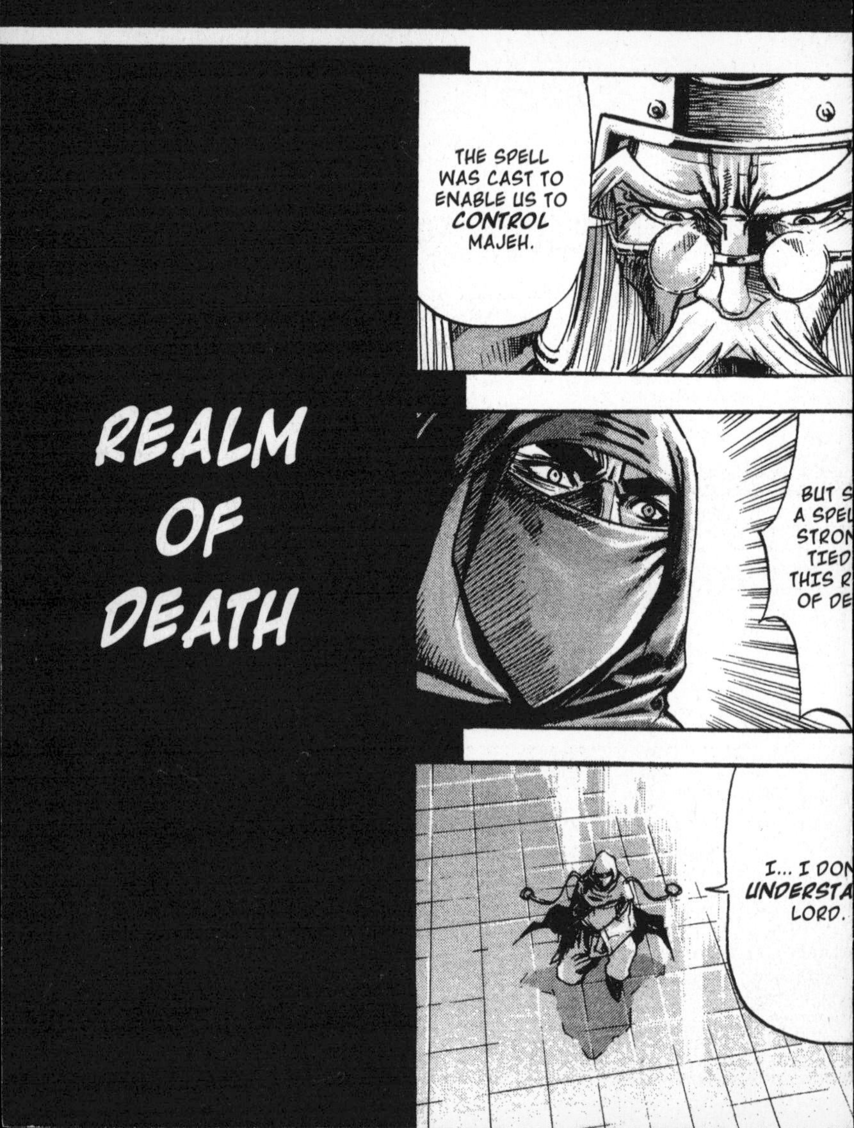

THE SPELL WAS CAST TO ENABLE US TO CONTROL MAJEH.
BUT S A SPEL STRON TIED THIS R OF DE
I... I DON UNDERSTA LORD.
REALM OF DEATH

STRENGTH SUPPRESSING ELL THAT HAS LED TO HIS EFEAT IS WOVEN FROM E UNIQUE ENERGIES OF THE NEXT WORLD. SO IT OULD STAND TO REASON HAT THE SPELL'S POWER OULD WEAKEN IN THE WORLD OF MORTALS.
THE RESTRAINING POWER OF THE SPELL IS IN TURN LINKED TO THE POWER OF MAJEH'S STRONG LIFE ENERGY. AS LONG AS HE CONTINUES TO LIVE-- THE SPELL WILL REMAIN IN FORCE.
THEN...NOW THAT HE IS NEAR DEATH...

YES. NOW TH
MAJEH'S LIFE
ABOUT TO B
EXTINGUISH
...THE SPELL WILL BE BROKEN!!

이이
번쩍
아아아아

IN THE NEXT VOLUME OF

KING OF HELL

you thought Majeh
as formidable before,
st wait 'til you see
m without the
perhuman Strength
aling Symbol holding
m back!
ne Tournament may
ve been interrupted,
it the real show's
bout to start!

ALSO AVAILABLE FROM TOKYOPOP®

MANGA

.HACK//LEGEND OF THE TWILIGHT
@LARGE
ABENOBASHI: MAGICAL SHOPPING ARCADE
A.I. LOVE YOU
AI YORI AOSHI
ANGELIC LAYER
ARM OF KANNON
BABY BIRTH
BATTLE ROYALE
BATTLE VIXENS
BRAIN POWERED
BRIGADOON
B'TX
CANDIDATE FOR GODDESS, THE
CARDCAPTOR SAKURA
CARDCAPTOR SAKURA - MASTER OF THE CLOW
CHOBITS
CHRONICLES OF THE CURSED SWORD
CLAMP SCHOOL DETECTIVES
CLOVER
COMIC PARTY
CONFIDENTIAL CONFESSIONS
CORRECTOR YUI
COWBOY BEBOP
COWBOY BEBOP: SHOOTING STAR
CRAZY LOVE STORY
CRESCENT MOON
CROSS
CULDCEPT
CYBORG 009
D•N•ANGEL
DEMON DIARY
DEMON ORORON, THE
DEUS VITAE
DIABOLO
DIGIMON
DIGIMON TAMERS
DIGIMON ZERO TWO
DOLL
DRAGON HUNTER
DRAGON KNIGHTS
DRAGON VOICE
DREAM SAGA
DUKLYON: CLAMP SCHOOL DEFENDERS
EERIE QUEERIE!
ERICA SAKURAZAWA: COLLECTED WORKS
ET CETERA
ETERNITY
EVIL'S RETURN
FAERIES' LANDING
FAKE
FLCL
FLOWER OF THE DEEP SLEEP
FORBIDDEN DANCE
FRUITS BASKET
G GUNDAM
GATEKEEPERS
GETBACKERS
GIRL GOT GAME
GIRLS' EDUCATIONAL CHARTER
GRAVITATION
GTO
GUNDAM BLUE DESTINY
GUNDAM SEED ASTRAY
GUNDAM WING
GUNDAM WING: BATTLEFIELD OF PACIFISTS
GUNDAM WING: ENDLESS WALTZ
GUNDAM WING: THE LAST OUTPOST (G-UNIT)
GUYS' GUIDE TO GIRLS
HANDS OFF!
HAPPY MANIA
HARLEM BEAT
HONEY MUSTARD
I.N.V.U.
IMMORTAL RAIN
INITIAL D
INSTANT TEEN: JUST ADD NUTS
ISLAND
JING: KING OF BANDITS
JING: KING OF BANDITS - TWILIGHT TALES
JULINE
KARE KANO
KILL ME, KISS ME
KINDAICHI CASE FILES, THE
KING OF HELL
KODOCHA: SANA'S STAGE
LAMENT OF THE LAMB
LEGAL DRUG
LEGEND OF CHUN HYANG, THE
LES BIJOUX
LOVE HINA
LUPIN III
LUPIN III: WORLD'S MOST WANTED
MAGIC KNIGHT RAYEARTH I
MAGIC KNIGHT RAYEARTH II
MAHOROMATIC: AUTOMATIC MAIDEN
MAN OF MANY FACES
MARMALADE BOY
MARS
MARS: HORSE WITH NO NAME
MINK
MIRACLE GIRLS
MIYUKI-CHAN IN WONDERLAND
MODEL
MY LOVE
NECK AND NECK
ONE
ONE I LOVE, THE
PARADISE KISS
PARASYTE
PASSION FRUIT
PEACH GIRL
PEACH GIRL: CHANGE OF HEART
PET SHOP OF HORRORS

TOKYOPOP®

SHE CAN PROTECT HER BROTHER FROM THE WORLD—
CAN SHE PROTECT THE WORLD FROM HER BROTHER?

www.TOKYOP